A PROMISE OF HOPE

A Collection of Poetry

Anthony Frobisher

In support of

Your local children's hospice

In loving memory of

Jewel April Arin Frobisher

18th April 2006 – 5th May 2006

And

Milla Chloë Arin Frobisher

20th April 2006 – 13th December 2016

For

For my wife Rini, daughter Louisa

For my mother Donna

For always giving me hope

Do not lose hope, nor be sad.
Al-Quran 3:139

Hope is being able to see that there is light despite all of the darkness.
Archbishop Desmond Tutu

Your choices reflect your hopes, not your fears
Nelson Mandela

Hope is the thing with feathers that perches in the soul - and sings the tunes without the words - and never stops at all.
Emily Dickinson

Even if the hopes you started out with are dashed, hope has to be maintained.
Seamus Heaney

Foreword

"The way in which a children's hospice delivers its mission depends greatly on the support of many people, all of whom bring their own perspective. The parent's perspective is unique and Tony's experience of Acorns with his daughter Milla have, for some years, led to a desire and drive to ensure that other families have access to the special care and support that Acorns offers families when they most need it. Whether on a bike travelling hundreds of miles to raise funds, live-streaming a sponsored guitar marathon, or in crafting and publishing such personal and poetic reflections, Tony remains a hugely valued fundraiser, speaker, and advocate for Acorns Children's Hospice. We are proud to have Tony as a Parent Carer Champion which helps others understand just a little of what a children's hospice is.

When our charity tries to explain what it does every day it is often best described by those who have been with Acorns and experienced first-hand how hard we work to make every day count for families. Making memories, offering emotional support, making sense of things, articulating and helping. In fact everything that poetry offers us. Bringing together positive reflections in this latest collection of his own poems and guest poets, we are thrilled to be the beneficiaries of 'A Promise Of Hope' and thank Tony and his special contributors for their gifts to Acorns."

Trevor Johnson

Chief Executive, Acorns Children's Hospice

3

Introduction

A Promise of Hope

What is hope? A feeling, an expectation, a desire? A dream, a possibility, a reality?

For me, hope is the freshness after rain, the first snowdrops that push through winter soils, and the gentle warmth of sunshine on a cold winter day.

But hope is also a connection. It is the smile of a stranger, a kind word from a friend, the simple words, 'how are you?' For the human experience is one of hopes, raised and dashed, realised and frustrated, triumphant highs and devastating lows.

Our daughters were born out of hope. Jewel, Louisa and Milla. My wife Rini and I hoped for children for 7 years. Without success. A course of IVF provided us that glimmer of light; hope, slim yet possible. Hope became reality and my wife became pregnant after only one IVF cycle. But with triplets came complications.

At only 24 weeks, my wife was rushed to Liverpool Women's Hospital, 125 miles from our home in Worcester. Jewel was born two days before Louisa and Milla. Sadly, Jewel passed away after only 17 days.

Our world imploded. But we had to remain strong and cling to the hope that Louisa and Milla would survive against the odds. Each baby weighed between 630g and 660g. Their chance of survival was very low. Yet, we hoped.

After 6 months in hospital, operations on their eyes, an operation to correct a hole in Louisa's heart, and numerous setbacks, our twins came home. Thanks to the skill, dedication and care of the wonderful Neonatal consultants, doctors and nurses at Liverpool Women's Hospital. Our hopes raised again that our children would grow and develop as other children do.

We knew Louisa had suffered complications due to detached retinas, a result of extreme prematurity. Only the skill of her surgeon saved her eyesight. He operated twice in two weeks, using lasers, to try to correct her problems. Louisa is blind in one eye and has partial sight in her other. Milla was much more fortunate with her eyesight.

Within a year we learned that Milla had developed severe spastic quadriplegia cerebral palsy. Her traumatic early birth had caused brain injuries which meant she was unable to walk or talk and required 24 hour a day care. She was fed through a gastrostomy, stomach tube.

Hope. The soaring highs and the saddest lows.

As a parent your hopes are that your children grow, learn, are happy, well educated, well rounded, successful people, forging careers and living their lives to the fullest. Disability has a way of crushing those hopes. We didn't let it.

Despite everything; the exhaustion, sleepless nights, the difficulties, mentally, emotionally and physically of caring for disabled twin girls, we never lost hope. Coupled with a strong faith, a determination to give our daughters the best start in life and to continue as they grew.

Louisa has mild developmental delay, meaning she has educational difficulties. Yet she is bright, articulate, happy, inquisitive, creative and at 17 on the verge of entering her young adult years. We have hope she achieves all she wants in life.

Milla smiled. Every day. Her smile gave us reassurance and hope. She couldn't talk (except saying Mum, yeah, *wuv yu*...love you). She struggled with illness, chest infections, frequent hospitalisations. She had numerous operations on her stomach and her legs But still she smiled.

In December 2016, on a visit to my wife's family in Indonesia, Milla became ill very suddenly. She passed away from a sepsis infection. Unexpected, sudden, devastating. She was only 10 years old.

Our world collapsed.

Hope no longer existed, only darkness and sadness.

We returned home to the UK a family of three. Milla was buried next to her grandfather in a cemetery in a small town on the island of Java. Jewel is buried 125 miles away in Liverpool.

You cling to hope until your fingers can no longer grip and you fall, in despair, plummeting.

How do you come to terms with such overwhelming loss? A daily routine filled every minute with administering medicines, setting up milk feeds by gastrostomy, sitting up all night trying to calm and coax an overexcited Milla whose body won't regulate sleep. Then an all-encompassing silence, time on your hands. Time when thoughts and memories flood you with grief.

The love and care of family, of friends, of health care professionals, so many people who rallied round. And Acorns Children's Hospice too.

Milla had regular respite stays at Acorns for the Three Counties in Worcester, allowing her the chance to enjoy herself and be well looked after by specialist nurses and volunteers in a safe, friendly, welcoming environment. It gave us the chance to reset and recharge, to relax and rest. They were a lifeline for us.

When we lost Milla, Acorns were there also. They reached out, provided a sympathetic, understanding ear, a shoulder to cry on and a promise we would always be part of their family and always welcome at the hospice.

Hope renewed.

The dark days do pass and hope reemerges like blossom on barren branches in springtime.

I began fundraising in 2007 for a number of charities. I found it cathartic and something that gave me a focus and a way of giving back. When we lost Milla I promised I would continue to fundraise in her memory.

Since 2007 I have raised over £50,000 for various charities including Acorns. I have climbed Kilimanjaro, trekked to Everest, cycled John O'Groats to Lands End, run the London Marathon, walked the length of the Worcester to Birmingham Canal in a day (33 miles), and crossed the Cotswolds (53 miles) in a day.

I have also done less strenuous fundraisers – 12 hours playing guitar and singing during the lockdown, as well as writing and publishing two charity cookbooks and poetry books.

Poetry was my way of channelling my emotions and expressing my grief. Losing Milla was a catalyst to my poetry.

In 2020 I wrote Let The Acorns Grows, a collection of my poems and supported by well-known poets such as Brian Bilston, Dean Wilson and Francesca Martinez. It raised around £300 for Acorns. In 2021 I wrote four separate books for A Poem A Day 2021 – over 400 poems in total. Each book raised money for a different charity, including Acorns Children's Hospice.

I was honoured and delighted to carry the Queen's Baton for the Commonwealth Games in Birmingham in 2022 in recognition of my fundraising for Acorns. I am currently a Parent Carer Champion for the charity, a role that allows me to educate others about the incredible work Acorns does and to give hope to others.

A Promise of Hope will also support Acorns. A place of kindness, friendship, care, love and of course, hope.

I hope you enjoy the poems in this collection.
Best wishes,

Tony Frobisher
Worcester
June 2023

Contents

Page

Poetry Chapters

All photographs by Anthony Frobisher
Cover photograph: Sunrise, Norton, near Worcester

©*Anthony Frobisher*

Title   **Page**

*All poems by Anthony Frobisher, except guest poems marked**

A Promise
of Hope

Hope

A Promise of Hope

The thinnest strands of first-light.
The half second as the sun lifts above the horizon.
The sliver of blue sky amongst the clouds.
The warming apricity as the wind drops.
The momentary cessation of the rains.
The increasing distance of lightning and thunder reply.
The first trickles of snowmelt.
The emergence of the first snowdrops.
The slow lengthening of days.
The noticeable swell of birdsong.
The new budding on the magnolia trees
The leaf return as forests reawaken
The scuffles of recently woken hedgehogs.
The first sightings of swift and swallow.
The first smiles of the grieving.

A promise of hope.

Absence and Presence

In Morning
I wake to your absence,
Thick as November fog.
Enveloping, restricting, impenetrable.

In Daytime
I feel your absence,
Keen as February winds.
Piercing, sharp, pained.

In Dreams
I sleep with your presence,
Vivid as May sunlight.
Tangible, palpable, here.

Sirens

When the sirens stop
The birds begin their song,
Defiant and unbowed.
And the winds die to
Inaudible whispers.

When the sirens stop
Hope slowly returns.
Spreading like sunrise
Over fields of sunflowers,
Under peaceful blue skies.

За Україну / For Ukraine

Слава Україні! Slava Ukraini! Glory to Ukraine!

*The madness in Ukraine continues. Senseless brutality, needless loss of life.
And yet, defiance, resilience, courage against a mighty enemy. What an
incredibly proud and resilient people the Ukrainian people are.
One day the sirens will stop.*

Drops of Hope

The first drops of rain
Upon parched and dusty earth.
Hope is renewed.

The last drops of rain
Upon flooded swollen fields.
Hope is renewed.

Changing Hopes

Hope is
The colour of spring.

Hope is
The warmth of summer.

Hope is
The beauty of autumn leaf.

Hope is
The first falls of winter snow.

At Sea, By Water

Sea Peace

Waves break the

       Silent shore, littered

With memories and

       Rock pool treasures,

That delighted faces

       Sparkling in the hues

Of sea glass shimmers

       And reflections now

Mirrored in the waves,

       Palette blue above and

Bottle green below.

       Where the rhythm flows

Upon happy tides and

       Sands shift with

Drifting current time

       For the sea peace.

Time for the sea peace.

You'll Find Me
(Sea Memories)

You'll find me
Where oceans
Spill across
Pebbled shores
In crack and clatter
And gentle swoosh.

You'll find me
Where the sea
Dances in white
Spray wave tops
That rhythmic repeat,
Crash, crash and return.

You'll find me
Under the greying skies
And bottle green waters,
Listening to the gulls
Speak of warmer days,
Cawing above the winds.

You'll find me
At the end of the pier,
Watching the horizon ships
Pass in silent distance.
While I listen for the sea memories
Borne on wind, wave and tide.

Spring Sea March

I watch the sea unfurl
And shore stretch, painting
The sand with foam fingers.
Rearranging the pebbles
With each pulse and break.
And wind-topped white horses
Ride the sea in great gallops,
The final play of winter.
I stand in the dawn light and
Welcome the rising tides of March,
Sea-change from dull-grey to bottled-green.
Spring waves with new warmth as
Winter ebbs to the north current.
Cold soaks into the empty shore
Buried deep until autumn's return,
Replaced by a hopeful sun.

I watch the birds swoop and sing,
Spring coast waits its Terns,
Kittiwakes and Guillemots,
Cliff perched in riotous crowds.
The wave bobbers and sea bombers,
Watching the beach horizon from afar.
Carried by the south currents
And feeling the warmth on their backs.
I stand as the first sunrise of spring
Marches skyward, a parabola of hope.
Casting gentle shadows over the sand
And damp pebbles reflect my happiness.
The water wraps itself around my ankles
And I feel its urgent tug, cold still.
The sea rarely warms itself to the task,
But the sun will bear witness to a happy Spring.
And warmth will return.

A Winter Pier

Salt haired and chapped lipped.
The high winter tide crescendo
Thudding against the stanchions.
A slow walk on the infinite pier,
The end unreachable, unneeded.
A look, comforting, secure.
A sea love story that began
On that same aging pier.
That well-worn bench.
The same well-worn bench,
Repainted but still redolent
Of the past, happiness and
Tentative dates, furtive glances.
Hands warmed in hands
Face to red-tinged face
Wind lashed, whipped or
Flushed from first kiss?
Shivering as the cold
Chased away the glow.
Shuddering with each
Wave, and myriad emotions.
Turning back into the
Teeth of the gale,
Still warmed by the
Presence of the other.
Cold left behind with the years.
And the end of the pier still
Unattainable, unreached.

Sea Grief

We called the seabirds.
Swooping and squawking -
The wave bobbers in
Constant chatter, exchanging
Stories in braggadocio caws,
Carried on playful winds.

And the seabirds mocked our tears.

We called the waves.
Beach bound, unfolding-
Each one cascading their
Story, demanding to be heard,
Before being absorbed by
The grateful sands.

And the waves battered our souls.

We called the ocean.
Voluminous and resonant.
Seemingly empty, yet
Teeming with life and
Swimming with stories.
Channelled by endless currents.

And the ocean swallowed our happiness.

We called the sharks.
Our grey-fears that remained
Hidden, unfathomable,
Threatening to surface and
Devour us in frenzied grief.
But the sharks meant no harm.

They had stories of their own.

The Depths
(Return of the Whales)

Light glinted from
Surface sparkles
And sun flashes,
Which faded into
Darkness, sinking
In the silent depths.

We waited for the whale song.
Resonance that penetrates
And wraps itself
Around our souls
And harks to childhood.
Memories risen from the depths.

A plume, a tail fin, no fluke,
And the great whales returned.
Plaintive cries and mournful
Sounds echoed from the depths.
Surfacing and breaching memories.
Do the whales remember?

A temporary explosion of
Bulk and mass and joyful
Display and thunderous splash.
We're here the whales said
And yes, we recall that happy child.
From the depths of our memory.

A Pebble for Your Thoughts

We stand imbibing the salt air,
Imbued with warmth.
A stillness under a
Summer sky reflected in
The lap and lull, the languid
Forth and back of lazy waves,
Breaking in soft cursive strokes
Across a shoreline where every
Pebble is a face, a smile,
A cheer, a laugh, a moment.
A memory contained.

The waves agitate pebbles
And a thousand voices begin to
Clatter and click in collective chatter,
Eager to talk, eager to unburden.
Our smooth unweathered hands
Caress the smooth pebbles,
Skimming them in joyous bounds
On mirror glass days towards
The horizon haze and the thought, perhaps,
The champion pebble would go on
Forever and hole a passing ship.

Each pebble willing to be picked up
And thrown and lobbed and skimmed
And tossed and chucked and hurled.
Because upon the beach the pebbles
Lay dormant, unthinking, unresponsive.
Only when re-immersed in the current,
The sea-shine, can they release their memories.
So that wave upon waves could return those

27

Precious thoughts to the beach where we wait,
Listening to the pebbles, hoping
But not understanding a word.

Until the waves gently engulf us,
Until we taste the memories on salt lips.
Until we are soaked in memories once more.

Flooded

Silent, stood by the
Current swirl and rapid flow.
Flooded with thoughts.

A moment to pause,
While ceaseless waters rush.
Flooded with memories.

The river swollen, pours
Pain channelled, mercury heavy.
Flooded with sadness.

Crisp air, sharp inhaled
By river's cold beating heart.
Flooded with tears.

Dusk lights silver glint;
The waters invite reflection.
Flooded with hope.

The waters are now still.
The mind flows in gentler streams.
Flooded with life

Night and Day

Light and Dark

Light

Light passes to dark
A disappearance into black
But light e'er remains

Dark

Darkness smothers as
Light fades to memories and
A promised return

Nadir and Zenith

I am enveloped in an
All-encompassing darkness,
That flows in my veins,
Treacle-thick, while
The heart beats and beats
Quicker and heavier, palpable.
A heart exhausted by the
Unfathomable depths of despair.
And surface thoughts are muted
By the arrival of the nadir.
By the disillusionment of hope.

I am chrysalis wrapped,
Shrouded in the words
Of others, words that resonate -
An inner vibration that
Generates unending warmth,
A reappearance of light.
And guiding hands that support,
Lift, carry, while faces unblur.
Gentle smiles elevate, resuscitate.
I breath again and blink in the zenith.
I blink in the presence of hope.

Sunset Light

Then fades the light,
While heartbeats soften
As dusk quietens thoughts.

A gentle, silent light
Joins the myriad colours,
A painted sunset sky.

The end of light,
Reflect the day!
And stillness becalms.

Breathe in the last light.
Keep the glow within so
Darkness will not follow.

Earth and Moon

The Earth asked the moon
If it ever felt alone
And the moon replied
It never showed its dark side

Moon Gazing

We gazed upon the
Crescent moon, newly risen.
Carving quiet hope.

Followed by the Moon

A path where
The moon rose
In hues of soft-silk,
Silvered grey-tones
Against the night-dark.

A black-patina canal
And the moonwake
Outwitted the star-shine,
Following the night-walker's
Rhythmic soft-steps.

A moment's pause
Before the moonglow
Gave way to dawn-light.
As thoughts moon-reflected,
Then walked on in silver-light.

The Moon and The Gulls

The moon traces
Silver scars across
A silent seascape.
The wind holds
Its breath now the
Gulls have gone,
Carrying memories
Beyond the horizon line.
Resting out the night,
Lulled by the swell
Of blackened waves
That court moonbeams.
A temporary reveal,
A silver flash that
Tricks the gulls
To fish and flail.
The gulls return empty
Once moonlight fades.
And memories are
Once more lost at sea.

The Language of the Moon

Chiaro di luna	Brillante speranza per il domani.
Mondlicht	Leuchtende Hoffnung für morgen.
Clair de lune	Brillant espoir pour demain.
Luz de la luna	Esperanza brillante para el mañana.
Moonlight	Shining hope for tomorrow.

Nocturne

A night filled with song,
An elegy for the day.
Refrain for 'morrow.

Prelude

Daybreak prelude
Dawn's exquisite crescendo
Piano sunrise

D.C. al Fine ♬

Of Nocturnal Melody

An open window.
A Chopin nocturne,
C Sharp Minor.
Delicate swirling air,
Perfumed by music.
The night's heat
Cooled and soothed
By unseen hands.
Piano, mezzo forte,
Forte, crescendo, then
Diminuendo, pianissimo, a
Refrain, softly repeated.
Balm to hearts
And troubled minds,
Until silence and
The applause comes
With the quiet
Of the night.
And the tears
Of all who
Stopped to listen.

Three Minutes After Midnight

00:00
Count the silence between
The twelve strikes, as midnight resonates
Where the streets are silent and empty.
And the clouds gather unseen,
As darkness obscures them.

00:01
Listen to your heartbeat.
A second between each beat,
A night-rhythm, no longer a
Daytime pounding to stress and noise.
Now a gentle trace, pulsing with silence.

00:02
Close your eyes and open
Your soul to dreams, a world
That waits for you. Unlock
The silent doors and enter
Your unconscious thoughts.

00:03
Breathe in. The soft, slow
Rise and fall, chest lifting
Imperceptibly, eyelids beginning
To gently flicker. Who knows what
Dreams you will remember.

No Time For Dreaming
(Northern Hope)

Walking soft steps along
A silent path in the
Cool of the small hours.
A slight fading of the light,
Still basking in the
Glow of the Midnight Sun.
Inhaling the night-breath.
No time for dreaming.

The wind has died and
Wisps of last clouds
Scud overhead, bound for
Other lands where the
Not-yet-a-sleepers
Wait for shorter days,
Counting the passing hours.
No time for dreaming.

Here darkness does not exist,
All sadness is carried away
On kind currents, evaporated
By the long-light in the
Arctic summer, warming,
Incongruous, unending, returning
Smiles from the midnight walkers.
No time for dreaming.

Silence accompanies every
Night-breath and slow step.
Waves continue to break on
The distant illumined beach,
A night-time pulse under a sky
Reluctant to darken, at peace.

We pocket the midnight sun.
No time for dreaming.

Our hands fold and
Fingers interlock,
Sealing this moment of
Ever-light, of memories
Made under the Midnight Sun.
Sadness and darkness won't come.
For now we are at peace.

A time for dreaming.

Night-Morning Sky

There's moonglade on the water.
Ammil sparkles under the darkness,
Caught in the night shine
Of star pricked skies.

The night breathes in crystals and
Frost steps trace an even stride,
Past the undisturbed swans,
Huddled in cosy reed nests.

The small hours are at a close
And the faintest grey light
Emerges on the dawn horizon,
The sky coloured with reluctance.

Along the canal the water casts
Black reflections from
A patina of gossamer ice
And every exhalation shimmers.

Under the yellow glow of dulled
Street lights atop quiet bridges,
The bricks suck in the cold,
Absorbing the gelid night.

Soft sounds, a lightness of foot and
Gentleness of breath mixing with the
First stirring of psithurism,
The new wind waking tree and leaf.

Spindrift glints in the moonwake.
The chill path is no longer mine, now

Warmed by early risers and steaming joggers,
Silence broken by faint bells from dog collars.

A deep inhalation and the night pours
Into greedy lungs, coughing up cold.
I leave a few final footprints in the frost
The night is fading, there is hope of sun.

And I walk, ignoring the cold that
Remains a stubborn companion.
I walk, guided by the last moonlight,
Eager for the warmth of home.

Night to Day

Where the day ends and the night is found,
A plaintive cry, a haunting sound, wrapped
In the dark winds, carried on the air.
The light has gone, left in despair, yet

Where the night ends and the day returns
Darkness lifts and our hearts yearn, cracked
With the dawn, the light, hope implied.
The dark has gone, the pain subsides, yes

Where the night ends, the day remains.
The clouds dissipate, and pain, lacks
The power to penetrate, to infiltrate and scar.
The day is here as the night departs.

Dawn Haiku

Night dissipates and
Darkness is now scattered by
Hopeful dawn colours

Stillness persists in
The calmness and quiet of
Water's reflection

Paths slowly revealed
Uncovered by light's return
Shining on our dreams

Sky-Trails

Memories, held in contrails.
A momentary suspension
Left in the wake of you.
Thoughts dissipating
In a jet stream of
Yesterdays.

Seasons of Emotion

A Whisper of Spring

Spring, defiant.
The first whispers,
Snowdrop heads
Parapet in final frosts.

Magnolia bud and bloom,
Fresh and brightened hues.
Whites and flushed pinks.
The innocence of spring.

Dawn retreats to
Early sunrise, where the
Daffodils echo the sundance
In the new warmth.

May days, the appearance,
Of returning bluebell,
On hillsides, soft-swaying,
Redolent and triumphant.

Spring is here they say.
A natural declaration!
A floral cacophony.
No longer a whisper.

Spring Buds

Spring buds unfurled
To summer bloom.

Which one contained
Your silent smile?

Which was coloured
By your gentle heart ?

Which one remained
After you had gone?

Springs buds blossomed
Into memories of you.

Spring Haiku

The melting snows feed
Root and branch, bud and blossom.
Winter, spring forth.

The black and white of
Winter morphs slowly into
Multicoloured spring.

Music of spring.
Insects hum and birdsong plays,
Even flowers dance.

Daffodils delight.
Momentary dominance then
Bluebells supersede.

I'll meet you where the
Sunshine lights April streams and
Everyone whispers.

Spring tides and hopes rise.
Possibilities in waves,
Again and again.

As the days lengthen
Opportunities increase
And hope remains.

The pages turn in spring.
Chapters expand and minds fill
With warm summer desire.

Summer Haiku

We woke to summer.
Cloud wisps, blue sky clarity.
No change till autumn.

Summer colours are
Vivid yellows, blues and the
Grey mists of morning.

See swallows and swifts,
A return to warmer climes.
But so soon to leave.

Lunchtime in the park
Workers at rest, bathe and burn
Sunshine in their smiles

Pub garden with friends.
Tables full of anecdotes.
Comfort in laughter.

The beach beckoning
The swarming of day-trippers.
The beach disappears.

Family picnic.
Car windows steam like a flask.
Rainy Days-by-Sea.

Evening gathering,
Children play, oblivious.
Light at 10pm.

The Heat in Summer - Unprecedented

There was fruit rotting in the fields.
The pickers had not returned
And a sour stench filled the air,
Mingling with sweat.
The stifling, unprecedented heat
Made conversation mute,
While heads beat timpani rhythms
And every news bulletin talked of
How the heat was breaking all records again.

The children were out for the summer,
Schools closed and September a lifetime away.
Yet the streets were lockdown-empty.
Nothing stirred, only the thick boiling air
As empty buses trundled past.
Bored shop assistants twiddled thumbs as
Over-worked air conditioners creaked and moaned,
Dripping in sympathy with anyone daring to
Spend a few minutes outside.

Waves lapped at empty shores,
The beaches deserted save for the earliest of risers.
Jogging and dog walking as the sun broiled
Angrily on the horizon, orange aflame and seething.
The cool of spring mornings a memory,
Now the heat only tempered a touch, a temporary
Relief, but the tacit threat remained ready to surface.
Each morning stoking the midday furnace.
Who dares burns! Mad dogs! Englishmen!

And what of night, oh fiery night?
We sat long past midnight, listening to Pavarotti.
'Nessun Dorma!' None shall sleep!
And even the soothing tones of *Clair de Lune*
Mocked as the moon shone like quicksilver.

Molten, languid, laconic, absorbing and
Reflecting the ire of the sun.
Yet when sleep came, dreams cast us into
Flames and consumed us, restless, turning.

Yes, we burned that summer.
We melted into submission, retreating indoors.
We dreamed of escaping, holidays to cooler climes,
The Algarve, The Costa del Sol, The French Riviera,
The Greek Islands, The Canaries...
Britain burned, the unprecedented becoming the norm.
And the politicians argued and blamed one another
For failure and incompetence and a dereliction of duty.
And then it was finally autumn, and the winds and rain
and cold arrived.
And we forgot that unprecedented summer, as if it hadn't
happened.

Until the next summer and the sun rose aflame once more.

Autumn Haiku

Summer has now past,
Gone in the blink of an eye.
Open to autumn.

Mornings in darkness,
As we wait the rising sun,
Later every day.

The wind is howling.
Hunker down and watch the storm.
Autumn hurries in.

Now morning air's changed.
Summer warmth is a memory.
Welcome the first frost.

The leaves are turning
Lush green to vivid colour.
Such beauty in death.

Branches bare the scars.
Wind stripped, naked, desolate.
Life remains within.

The animals are gone.
Season's change, chill winds arrive.
Hibernation starts.

Autumn skies above.
Murmurs and movement southward.
The birds will return.

Leaf Falling, Autumn Passing

The leaves have been swept away.
Tidied into neat piles by autumn storms
And winter boots that shuffle with
The slowness of season's change.

Colour faded from splendid to dulled.
The spent leaves don't notice the
Approach of winter, inexorable and
Unstoppable, as the night fog lingers.

The trees are adding their annual ring,
Bark insulating against the cold march.
Spring and summer forgotten, as leaves
Drift into the frost strewn litter.

Above, sullen-sky cloud full
Raindrop weeps on bare branches
As autumn slowly swirls and drifts.
The leaves newly settle, not yet swept away.

Nature's Portent

Autumn teases
As warmth clings
To summer memories.
Perhaps it will last,
The final hurrah
Of Indian Summer.
Dazzling in purple, ochre
Gold and russet of
Turning leaves.
The pathways are
Littered with
Winter portent.
Leaf-fade, a dolour,
Ashen veined,
Scattered and jumbled,
Mulched and decaying.

Autumn stirs anew in
The first storms.
Albert, Beatrice, Cedric
Delilah, Edward etc.
Destroyers all,
Harbingers of dark days
And insufferable cold.
The moping months and
Misery-mouthed.
But the storms smile,
Wreaking havoc.
Deluge and flood,
Ice and blizzard.
Winter interminable,
As the colds wind
Scream gales of laughter.

Winter has outstayed
Its welcome. But won't leave.
Yet, turn the new year
And slow fades the
Long nights, glimmers
Of hope in a just perceptible
Change in the grey mornings.
Lightening, a fraction
Until the whole.
And snowdrops dance again.
And the sun sneaks its rise
Before you wake.
And the leaves unfold again,
Resplendent in new green.
Summer portent,
Winter soon forgotten.

Winter Haiku

Winter dawns silent.
Cracked ice and frosted pathways
And spring's distant dreams.

Workers dark depart.
A neon lit office day.
Workers dark return.

Wrapped up on cold days.
Friends talk in warm exchanges,
Words condensed in air.

The first flakes falling.
Delighted laughs of children.
Let's hope it settles.

Waking to silence.
The muffle of falling snow.
Children unaware.

A beach in winter,
Snow covered and pristine white.
Beneath summer waits.

Curtains drawn at 5.
Now the darkness settles in
For the long night shift.

Evening logs crackle.
Burning through happy memories
And tales of the day.

Seasonality

For Now I Am Winter

Spindrift thoughts.
Winter seeps through windows
As drafts hiss with the winds,
Swirling cold memories.
The bones are rattling
The marrow and teeth
Sing a frozen song.
I shiver in the last light.
For now I am winter
And the dark closes in.

For Now I Am Spring

Our breath no longer
Frost shimmering
In the cold dawn.
The new buds drip raindrops
Like happy heartbeats,
As petrichor fills the air
And mixes with blossom aromas.
Smiles appear on trees.
For now I am spring
And light is all around.

The Nature
of Things

The Song Walker

Footsteps in sand beats
Under a rhythm sun.
Where the lines stretch
From the dreamtime
And beyond the horizon.
Whispered mirage memories
Swallowed by the heat haze.

The songs have begun.
Each lifted to join with
The rare clouds drifting
In a languid dissonance
Over a land of Outback red.
Yet the music shimmers too,
Wind notes and earthen drum.

We measure distance by
Song lengths, counting verses
And stories shared, generations
Past in the lyrics and song-lines
Repeated refrains, the heat of words
Cooled by evening's sudden arrival
And tempered by unexpected desert rains.

A blessing in the music that
Accompanies each footstep.
Buoyed by melodies, strengthened
By hopes held, sustained by the rocks
That listen to the song walker.
The songs absorbed into cracks,
Striations that ripple echoed applause.

Listen to the forever songs.
Walk on song walker, walk on.
Forever the songs
Will guide you.
Walk on song walker, walk on.
Forever the songs
Will save you.

The Bookkeeper of Lahore

The door bell tinkled, opening to
An accompaniment of suffocating heat
And a cloud of dust motes dancing
In the early afternoon air, and the sweet
Smell of Raja Hameez's *jalebi* and *laddu*
Drifting in, perfuming the bookshop, infused
With delicate notes of cardamom and ghee,
The heady aroma of vats of *garam chai* tea.

The bookshelves were filled,
A sad sight for a bookseller.
For a bookseller is not a bookkeeper.
He wished he would sell a few more.
Kept books and full shelves meant empty pockets.
And a store empty of customers.
He cooled his brow with a damp cloth
Absorbing the sweat, then sweeping the dust
Disturbing the light and the gathering moths.

He couldn't recall the faces who bought the books,
But the books left his shelves like a first born leaving
home,
Trailing silence behind them and guilty looks.
Hemmingway to an earnest young student.
Edgar Alan Poe to a po-faced politician.
Kipling's Kim to a curious cleric.
Orwell's Down and Out in Paris and London
to a well-to-do member of the Lahori elite.
Each one a sale, a success, but also a defeat.

For every book that was packaged and sold,
Pristine and new or dog-eared, much read and old,
Was a listener, a confidante, a colleague, a friend,
A start at the beginning and read to the end.

A tale, a moral, a lesson shared and learned.
Knowledge acquired and praise richly deserved.
The bell tinkled, a new customer entered to browse the store.
Which book will he rip from the heart of

The Bookkeeper of Lahore.

Suspiration

A breath,
Suspiration.
Inhaling oceans
And mountains.
And the heady
Incense of spring
Woodlands and
Meadow flower.
A gentle exhalation,
Breath notes laced
With nature's gifts.

A breath,
Suspiration.
Inhaling daylight
And warmth.
And the freshness
Of summer evenings,
Cool night air and
The presence of silence .
A gentle exhalation,
Breath notes graced
With the promise of tomorrow.

Silent Whistles

Saturday starts
in silence,

The whistle
        of tinnitus,
The whistle
        of memories

Kettle poured into each moment.

Saturday starts
in silence,

The whistle
        of winter winds.
The whistle
        of soft breaths.

And even the memories

Whistle in
whispers.

Parade of Birds

The birds assembled for
Morning call, all present
And correct, ready to
Pass muster and
Salute the daybreak
With dawn songs.

At-ten-tion!

A chorus parade to the
Beats of soft wing.
By the light, quick march!
A twittering report,
Left, right, to the left
And to the right,
Birdsong plays on.
Then sparks the
Sun's slow return.
Regimented and
Precision rising.

At ease!

The birds fall out,
Duty called, duty done.
Another day begun.
The sun salutes back.
The dawn chorus
Bird parade.

Dismissed!

Karakoram Butterfly

The air was thin
And an evening wind brought
Glacial cold from the
Sharp peaks that glowed
Pink in the Karakoram sunset.

The road was riven by freeze thaw
And the rumble of heavily laden trucks,
China bound or Pakistan headed.
Potholes filled with fresh rains
And recent snow melt.

A flash of brown translucent wings,
Delicate and skittish, unexpected.
A Karakoram Banded Apollo butterfly
At home in the rarefied air,
Nature persists, we are but guests.

A lone figure approached in
Dark green shalwar kameez and
A beige woollen Hunza cap,
Flat like unleavened bread,
Atop a white-bearded head.

Eyes that pierced the gathering
Gloaming and shone with
Curiosity, warmth and presence.
'*Asalaam waalaikum* - Peace be Upon You!'
'Welcome to Pakistan,' with arms extended.

A smile that formed a gentle
Crescent moon framed by starlit eyes.
'How may I help you?' he enquired at
2,800m on a remote road, under peaks
That towered in imposing welcome.

We returned the greeting of peace
And thanked him for his kind welcome,
Assured him we were fine and taking in our
First breaths of a new country.
With a smile and a nod, he departed.

As silent and graceful as
A Karakoram butterfly.

Himalayan Echoes

We heard the echoes.
Splintered ice and cracked rock.
The high birds calling out
Warnings in dizzying circles.

We heard the echoes.
The thundering rumble of rockfall.
The ibex, stoic, unmoved, bleating
Warnings perched on near vertical cliffs.

We heard the echoes.
Avalanche rush of snow filled air.
The marmots in high pitch, whistling
Warnings while scurrying into burrows.

We heard the echoes.
Until the echoes fell silent and
There were no more warnings and
Only the gentle ringing of yak bells remained.

We Became Mountains

I stared into the abyss,
Crevasse drawn.
A beckoning darkness.
A cold embrace.
The hidden sun,
A lost warmth.

My face scarred, wearing
A carapace of sadness,
Solid, frozen, immovable.
My limbs numb, pained.
The ache of wounds
Sustained long before.

I wearied, afraid to fall,
Sapped and drained of will by
The punishing cold, unforgiving.
I could not go on, let me fall.
Let me surrender to cold and darkness.
Let me fall, let me fall.

A hand reached out,
Pulled me from the abyss.
Chiselled the sorrow from
My face, and rescued
A forgotten smile.
Let's climb he said.

We brothers held the rope
Of kinship and friendship,
Climbing together as one.
Our summits reached,
Each personal, different.
Yet we shared the same view.

Where friendship conquers
Fear and sadness and loss.
Where warmth of kindness spreads
Like sunrise and no cold penetrates.
Where we will never fall,
Secured, tethered to friendship.

I climbed, I failed.
But when we climbed
We succeeded.
I climbed and
was nothing.
But when
we climbed,
We became
mountains.

Inspired by a friendship and someone I greatly admire, Ellis Stewart, author of Everest: It's Not About the Summit and Misadventure: Lessons Learned From a Life of Ups and Downs

The Heart-Star

The fields were gilded
Under a vermeil moon.
And the stars hung
In quiet night time reverie.

The road was a black line
With sparkling frost.
And cold penetrated,
Quickening heartbeats.

A man and a young child craned
Their necks, angled towards
The infinite blackness, eyes illuminated
By the gentling moon.

Which star will you become?
Asked the child, staring
Transfixed up into myriad pinpricks
Of light dotting the welkin.

A star that is ever present,
Came the reply. Even on the
Nights hidden behind the saddest clouds,
My star will still shine brightly for you.

But how will I find it? the child asked,
Joining stars with their finger, in a
Celestial dot to dot. How will
I find your star when you're gone?

The man smiled and reached up,
Plucking a star. Here, open your hands.
Now hold them over your heart.
Let the light in and know it is me in you.

The child held their hands over their heart,
As the man held the child in a warming embrace.
Dad, the child said, you'll always be my star.
And you'll always be mine, he replied.

Whenever you try to find my star,
Look to the heavens and know every
Star is a memory of us, and know
You still carry that one special star

In your heart.

*A conversation about stars. For our children, we are all stars. Shine as brightly
as you can for them in all you do.*

*Written for and dedicated to the memory of a special man, taken too soon,
Rob Metcalfe.*

There is Silence

There is silence
In the rippling water
And each flick of fish tail.

There is silence
In the rustling reeds
And each note of birdsong.

There is silence
In the rushing wind
And each chirp of insects.

There is silence
In the rhythm-swaying wildflowers
And each butterfly touch.

There is silence
In the readying of nature.
There is silence.

We only need to listen.

Call Off Your Storm

Thoughts like anvil heads.
The thunder strikes before
The lightning, flashing
Across bloodshot eyes.
Bilious clouds bubble and
Trouble minds, dark, grey.
Call off your storm.

A deep depression
Spreading, overcast.
Weathered, beaten.
No hope for sunlight. It rose,
It rose! Somewhere light
Is present, yet dark persists.
Call off your storm.

Count the seconds, thunder-fade.
A glimmer of sky, pale, weak,
But present, emerging.
The deluge passes, raindrops
Glint, the first smiles return.
Petrichor-air fills the lungs.
Call off your storm.

Delicate Transitions

When did you first notice the lines that
Greeted every laughter had become a permanent fixture,
Even though you saw yourself every day?

When did you realise the face in the mirror had changed
From boy to man, girl to woman, young to middle to old-
aged,
Even though you did not feel it at all?

When did you understand that time is relentless,
Yet barely noticed, as soft as the ticking of a clock,
As rhythmic and silent as heartbeats?

When did you accept that we age every second,
Inexorably, imperceptibly, inescapably?
And such delicate transitions mark us, shape up

And define who we are.
For us to fail to notice
And for others to see.

A Wish

A wish is a
A gentle breeze,
A hand, a squeeze.
A quiet favourite place,
A long and needed embrace.
A freshly brewed cup of tea in a mug,
A smile hello how are you a warming hug.
A stroll along an evening sunset beach,
A memory there always within reach.
A bench to rest in warm summer air,
A look that says you'll always care.
A hill we climbed to stand on top,
A life we wish had never stopped.
A single flake of crystal snow,
A love that will eternally grow.
A place to go when tears fall.
A wish is you and that is all.

Refuge for the Refugee

A Pebble Beach
(Arriving in Waves)

A pebble beach.
A wave of emotion.
A welcome hand.
A tearful disbelief.

A silent smile.
A pebble beach.
A wave of relief.
A whispered prayer.

A sudden shiver.
A warm blanket.
A pebble beach.
A wave of grief.

A wave of memories.
A reassuring voice.
A hope for a future.
A pebble beach.

That Sinking Feeling

To flee conflict.
To escape persecution.
To be free to be who you are.

To stand on a shore.
To enter a boat.
To cross the sea.

To pray you survive.
To hope for a new life.
To want only to live.

But always surfacing.
The desperation, the worry,
The anxiety, the fear.

That
Sinking
Feeling.

Small Boats

Small boats
Full of fear and apprehension.
Small boats
Full of questions and confusion.

Small boats
Full of war and persecution.
Small boats
Full of death and destruction.

Small boats
Full of anxiety and desperation.
Small boats
Full of cold and exhaustion.

Small boats
Full of loss and sorrow.
Small boats
Full of yesterday and tomorrow.

Small boats

Full of silence and sadness.
Small boats
Full of inhumanity and madness.

Small boats
Full of life and humanity.
Small boats
Full of hearts and minds and identity.

Small boats
Full of a past lost to flames and smoke.
Small boats
Full of dignity, lives, people,

Small boats
Full of hope.

Beneath the Waves

Beneath the waves,
Where sunlight fades.
A silence, black and
Thoughts swirling,
Where darkness pervades
And storms rage unfelt,
We are lulled into
Dream states.
And waves
Cease.

Beneath the waves,
Where calm persists,
We return, climbing
Into the womb of
Memories, seeking
Stillness and peace.
A haven sought.
Reality wakes in
Harsh light.
No longer

Beneath

The

Waves

The Cliffs Are Not White

The cliffs are not white.
Do not let them deceive you.
No, the cliffs are not white.
We watch their towering presence.
They are the colour
Of welcome, of departure,
Of love and loss,
Of greeting and farewell,
Of sanctity, sanctuary and life,
Of sadness, despair and death.

The cliffs are not white.
Do not let them fool you.
No, the cliffs are not white.
They are different colours
to different people - they are
The grey of uncertainty,
The flecked green of hope,
The crumbling pale chalk of fragility,
The new-day pink of friendship,
The fading brown of impermanence.

The cliffs are not white.
Do not let them trick you.
No, the cliffs are not white.
Time has changed their hue
And colours taint each person's view.
They are the black of wartime,
They are the red, white and blue of victory,
They are the sea-green of history,
They are the ash-waves of the refugee,
They are the pebble-slate-clean of new opportunity.

The cliffs are not white.
Do not let them convince you
That they are white and will ever be.
For the cliffs are painted
With nature's palette,
With our memories and hopes,
With newcomers and forever leavers,
With our past and present and futures,
With all our experiences.

The cliffs are not white.
They are whatever colour
you wish them to be.

The Smile of A Child That Has Seen So Much

A child, wrapped in a
Worn, torn jacket.
Each tear a knife jab
A pained memory.
Ragged, despairing,
Heart-wrenching,
Scarring and indelible.
Mouth numbed, taut
Unspoken, silent.

A child, held in
Fearful shivering arms.
Cold-penetrated and
Salt-soaked with briny
Tears and ceaseless
Spitting waves.
Telling the child,
Don't be afraid.
It's almost over.

A child, lifted by
Strong, patient sea-arms,
A saviour and a boat.
Sat blanket wrapped and warmed.
Blanking the memories of
Home and loss and fear and war.
A kind face speaking
A language as yet unfamiliar.
A brief emotionless look in return.

A child, just a child.
Innocence burning in eyes
That have seen too much,
Know too much, and yearn so much

To hold the hand of a mother, father
That doesn't shake with fear.
A child, ashore, new land, language, hope.
A child held in the embrace of family.
A child who has not smiled for months,

Smiles once more.

We Walked

We walked over broken brick and glass,
Shattered fragments of recent lives
Lost to memories in burnt photographs,
But held in hearts that pulsed with pain
And minds defiled by war and hatred.

We fled, led by fear and chased by demons,
Passed through heartless, pitiless hands.
We flocked like flightless helpless birds
Crowding the shore, searching for hope
Between each trembling wave.

We left the solidity of dry land
For the uncertainty of the sea.
Life and death on a boat, a raft of hope?
Washed ashore by the endless tide
Of those that would follow us.

We arrived in the cold sunrise
Of a new dawn and the alien
Land that stretched before us was
Hope. But all that glitters can be tarnished
By rejection, mistrust, suspicion and hatred. Yet

We walked on foreign soil,
Embraced by foreign arms.
Listening to foreign voices,
Watching foreign faces,
Enjoying foreign tea and tradition.

We found hope. It was there
Shining in the cracks in the darkness.
And in the faces that smiled with welcome
And kindness that lit memories of home
And family and friendship.

91

We forgot despair for a few precious moments,
And walked with our foreign friends
Upon pebble beach and alien streets.
Drinking milky tea and imbibing soft words
From those who we now realised were not foreign,

Because they walked with us too.

The Human, Kind

AI did not buy flowers when we were grieving.
AI did not comfort and share gentle words.

AI did not enquire how we were, what we needed.
AI did not support us in the darkest times.

AI did not understand the raw emotions.
AI did not feel the anger, sadness, frustration, despair.

AI did not sense our need for silent reflection.
AI did not join us in the comfort of solace and prayer.

AI did not help to carefully rebuild our lives.
AI did not give us time and space to heal.

AI could never replace

The Human, kind.

Distance

The distance between us
Is the distance between stars.
The distance between us
May be shrouded in darkness.
The distance between us
May feel infinite and unfathomable.
The distance between us
Will always be illuminated
By the presence of you.
The distance between us
Will cease to exist while
Your memory still shines.

Heart Smiles

The smiles of strangers
Can lift the darkness from the
Most broken of hearts.

Greetings

Good morning, they said.
And the greeting stayed in the
Lonely heart all day.

Elevated

We languish in the
Lowest of valleys, yet crave
The highest mountains.

Interlude

Do we pause to remember the
Smiles of passing strangers?

Do we think and recall each
Act of thoughtful kindness?

Do we stop and appreciate
Everyone we know?

Do we take the time
To make time for others?

Do we create the interludes
In life to fill with all those we love?

Broken Pieces

Broken pieces.
Heart-scattered.
Life woven in the
Patterned tiles.
Still.

Broken pieces.
Shards and parts,
Life fragments,
Memory-lain.
Still.

Broken pieces
Regathered, recollected.
Life pieced together,
Heart-restored.
Moving.

You Stood

You stood, summit-spent.
Bloodshot eyes, with tears
Streaked on red-cold cheeks.
A raging gale sinking its
Bitter teeth and ripping
Flesh from your bones and
Freezing your marrow.

You stood, storm-bent.
Doubled against the fierce
Swirling memory-winds that
Pummelled you with sadness.
And etched your hurt in weathered-lines.
Cold-stung and grimacing
An unrelenting, unforgiving pain.

You stood and faced the torment,
And bore the storm wind.
A dignified air, resilient,
Unbowed and determined.
Come hammer the blows and beat you down!
But the cold-wind could never win.
You stood tall, a grimace returned to smile.

And only the wind died.

Peace Is...

Peace
Is the space
Between heart beats,
And the moments suspended
Between every in and exhalation.
And the flash of darkness in every blink.
The last second between sleep and waking,
And the lingering silence between soft words.
The counting between lightning and thunder
And the final blackness before daybreak.
The soothing interludes within birdsong,
And the calm in watching the sun rise.
The last dry moment before rainfall,
And the lull between gentle waves.
The expectancy before laughter
And tingles before an embrace
The hesitation in 'I love you'
And the quickening space
Between heart beats.

We Are The Same

We are the same,
Voices to be heard.
Minds to be free.
Kindness to be shared.
A need to be loved.

We are the same
Hearts that beat
With the pulse of life.
Quickening with our
Hopes and dreams.

We are the same.
No matter language or culture.
No matter faith or colour.
No matter place or country.
We are the same.

The Passing of Years

Window for a Child
(An Open Book)

An open book.
A window open
To a world that
Can be extraordinary,
Enriching, enlightening,
Entertaining, exciting.
Encapsulating dreams
And hopes and ambitions.
Encountering realities and
Fears and anxieties, yet
Overcoming challenges and
Difficulties with intelligence,
Humour, bravery and tenacity.
Windows that should always
Provide clarity of a worldview
And a voice for and of children.
Where words create lasting memories.
Where words mean so much.
Where words are everything.

The Pages of a Child

An old man stood
Watching a young child,
Sat still, hardly moving.
Undisturbed, soundless.

Only the gentle
Rise and fall of
Soft in and exhalations
Signalled their presence.

The old man
Stifled a cough,
Disturbing the child.
They turned, smiled.

'Grandad, what are you doing?'
'Watching you,' he replied.
'What are you doing?'
'Reading my new book.'

'That's grand, lad,' he said.
'I'll leave you to it.'
The child smiled and turned a page.
The old man lingered a moment.

He watched the boy turn another page.
'There's hope for us still,'
The old man thought.
There's still hope.

In Children's Eyes

In January dark, the year began where hope still quietly resides,
Heart carried, in gentle smiles, bright in children's eyes.

In February storms, the winds raged and angry roared outside,
Yet kindness and love quelled the fear seen in children's eyes.

In March the first fluttering of fragrant blossom skies,
A desire to breathe in the spring, reborn in children's eyes.

In April fell the rains, earth's sustenance required,
And the flowers nature-scent, a delight in children's eyes.

In May the bee collected pollen, buzzing with honeyed pride,
A golden skittering dance, sunshine lit in children's eyes.

In June we stared up at never ending blue horizon skies,
That reflected peace and calm, softly pooled in children's eyes.

In July seaside days and sun rays met on sandy beaches wide,
Laughter unfolding in crashing waves, joy in children's eyes.

In August summer mellowed and took its final stride,
The last evening's sun-hurrah, glowing in children's eyes.

In September fall gold, purple, russet leaves and nature died,
Yet nature will spring again a colour burst in children's eyes.

In October the nights were moon-blessed and star-scattered comprised,
As the first autumn frosts brought shivered morning-sparkles alive in children's eyes.

In November we woke cloaked in endless fogged morning reprise,
Yet the weakening sun still contained clarity and warmth found in children's eyes.

And in December the snow drifted silently, a welcome white surprise,
And the Christmas smiles of children, saw tears of pride snowflake fall, in all our quiet eyes.

A Portrait of a Poet as an Older Man

Youth flowed from smile lines and
Frown lines were crevassed,
Deepened by decades.

Teen passed to man to older man.
The colour of years now
Aged to white and grey.

What of the thoughts
And words of youth?
Were they superficial, trite, irrelevant?

No. Each word and sentence moulded
The wisdom of ageing,
Experience captured and stored in memories.

The heart beats, breaths taken,
Blink and the years pass by.
Age is seen, is worn, yet youth remains within.

The Voices

The voices began
With the sunrise.
Whispered mists
And chill breaths,
Waking in shivers.

The voices grew louder
In the morning air.
Dew fresh and condensed.
Encouraging, resonant,
Awakened and attentive.

The voices threatened
In the building heat.
Towering like thunder clouds.
Insistent, swelling,
Latent, potent, aggressive.

The voices dulled
In the wake of the storm.
Sky-cracked and spent.
Rain-soothed, gentling,
Lulled to repose.

The voices fell silent
In the calming sunset.
Awash with coloured thoughts,
Unafraid of approaching night,
Acceptance, at rest.

The Sounds of Loneliness

The television, blaring, a trite chattering.
The radio, playing, an unheard muttering.
The kettle, boiling, a solemn whistling.
The clock, ticking, an inevitable passing.

The phone, unanswered, an endless repeating.
The doorbell, pressed, a harsh ringing.
The letterbox, rapped, a metallic clattering.
The window, knocked, a dull thudding.

The voice, soft, a concerned greeting.
The friend, warm, a welcome hugging.
The tears, relieved, a gentle sobbing.
The silence, broken, a longed-for speaking.

The Cat in the Window. Still

A dusty window sill,
Sunlit and dappled beams.
From where the widow quietly watches.
And still believes, and still sees.
And where the cat, wizened in sunlight warmth, sleeps.
So still its breath barely disturbs the thickening dust.
Youthful once, in leaping bounds
Now faded silver and dusted grey.
With movements, slow and unhurried,
Its tail flicks near imperceptible,
Joining the tick of an unseen clock,
Ears ever alert and pricked
At the strike of every quarter hour.

Milky eyes, cataract closed.
Yet its limpid dreams are those of the widow,
Whose heart gently purred as her husband
Stepped wearily through the gate
And walked through that happy door,
As night shifted into dawn.
The joyful hour upon work's return
And a smile that warmed with
The smell of fresh baked bread,
Clinging to cloth and skin and breath.

But the door no longer opens
And the fish scraps are no longer scattered in a bowl.
As the cat weaved expectantly,
In delighted figures of eight,
And pawed at his spindly legs,
Ill-fit in an oversized factory uniform.
The door no longer opens,
Save for the cat on rarish days.
Outside seldom beckons.

A preference in age,
For comfort stays
And lies still,
On that dusty window sill.
And the sighs and purrs are mournful..
Its dreams are those of the widow,
Sat gathering dust.
Waiting for the door to open again.
Watching. The cat in the window.
Still.

The Songs of Caged Birds

In the courtyard a few caged birds are singing
Beautiful, desperate, plaintive songs.
Melodious calls, hoping for freedom.
Can anyone find beauty in a caged bird?

Shouldn't all birds be free from entrapment?
Shouldn't we open their doors to freedom?
Ah, but they would have little hope of surviving.
And cats would pounce as they fell, unable to fly on
weakened wings.

Or perhaps they would die of starvation,
Far from the forests they truly belong.
Their songs silent and lifeless.
But shouldn't they sing in freedom, even the once?

Is it better a life of unending imprisonment, or
Is it better the possibility, the proximity of death, or
Is it better to end suffering in the hope they may,

Just may,

Survive.

Same...Different

I left the warm house
I left the damp doorway
I walked to the station
I walked to the station
I sat on a cold bench
I sat on a cold street
I read the newspaper
I read the blank faces
I boarded the train
I heard the trains
I sat surrounded by strangers
I sat surrounded by strangers
I watched the commuters bored with life
I watched the commuters still alive
I joined the throng along the street
I joined no one as I watched their feet
I saw the man
I saw the man
I almost ignored his street-worn face
I almost turned away in embarrassment
Peter? I asked
John? I replied
Same school
Same class
Same teacher
Same friends
Same university
Same course
Same graduation
Same celebration
Same see you soon
Same 'til we meet again
Same person
Same street
Same people
Different lives.

Thoughts

England-by-the-Summer

10am
The car parks are full,
The late arrivals circling like
Vultures preying for a free space.

10:30am
The ice cream shops have queues
Ten deep, running low on 99 flakes
And mint choc Cornettoes.

11am
The tourists flock to cafe and shop
And arms aloft in a sea of selfies.
Memory clicks ready for the gram.

11:30am
The benches are all taken with
Weary backsides and a thousand questions about why
They decided to come here on a Sunday in June.

12pm
The cafes hum with knife and fork
And talk and clatter and shatter the peace of
An English village in summertime.

12:30pm
Tears and tantrums from tired
Toddlers dropping ice cream cones and chips.
While seagulls and dogs fight over pavement morsels and
titbits.

1pm
The souvenir shops fridge magnets
Pull the tourists in
And no one buys postcards anymore.

1:30pm
Lunch perfumes the thronging streets.
Tempting smells of overpriced eats.
At least the coffee's good.

2pm
Faces, pink, puce and singed
And shoulders burnt to a crisp.
Knees plead to be covered up.

2:30pm
Hats and poses, smiles and cheese
In Chinese, Spanish and Dutch.
Overseas and over here and overjoyed.

3:00pm
Escape the herd and head for home.
Another trip to England-by-the-Summer.
There's nothing better.

And of course we'll return.
We always do.

England-by-the-Sea
(Summer Voices)

The beach scattered in a thousand tongues,
Guttural, tonal, rhythmic under the English sun.
Where French mixes with an Arabic flair,
The Pole and Latvian gazing in horizon stares.
And the Czechs and Indians wolf down 99's,
As the Russians and Turks while away their time,
In amusement arcades where
Machines flash, whir and bing,
A coined unity, let the summers sing,
In Greek and Urdu and Lithuanian voice,
Gather the beach flock, by happy choice.
Where hijab smiles mix with tattooed chests
And yarmulkes laugh next to beer bellied flesh.

The Wetherspoons hum to knife and fork clatter,
As the Chinese, Japanese and Koreans chatter
And savour their beer battered cod,
A pint of lager, a packet of crisps
And the old timers are lost
In memories of summers before the
Day-trippers and tourists were rife.
When the town was in ruin, run down,
Decrepit, devoid of life.
Where the drab, grey streets were filth and litter cast,
Graffitied shelters, beer can strewn and shattered glass.
But now they pour into this quiet seaside town,
In every colour; sunburnt pink, black and brown
Fortunes restored among the flower beds
And hustling, bustling pier,
Washed in on a global tide from far and near.

On the promenade the Spaniards saunter
And Germans stride,
The Filipinos lick sugar from lips and doughnuts,
Hot, greasy, freshly fried.
And every face is a day, a smile, time by the sea,
And every voice is the music of diversity.
A sea song in waves of commonplace,
Witness the seagull observant but not a trace
Of hostility towards those on joyful day trips.
He cares not if the droppers of chips
Speak English, Portuguese, Yoruba or Malay,
Life is as one on English seaside days.
And as the sky fades and the sun finally sets,
Every face and voice fades too,
Fades to a happy silhouette.

Homesick Ex Patria
(Thinking of Britain)

Teatime

Tea's made, open the biscuit tin.
Digestive, Bourbon, Garibaldi,
Help yourself, dive right in.

Inaccurate Forecast

Cloudy, cold, rain in the air.
Heavy coat, gloves and hat, yet
The first sun in weeks, happy respair.

Oh It's Raining

Sudden storms, wind battered squalls
Picnic flooded, sandwiches sodden
Sans umbrella and soaked to the core

Attention All Shipping

The Shipping Forecast, all at sea.
Tyne, Dogger, Fisher, Bight.
Gales 4-5 moderate good in Cromarty .

Sporting Moments

Test Match Special, Match of the Day.
FA Cup full time giant killings,
The games that we play.

Hear Hear

PMQs Mr Speaker addressed.
Front and back benches.
The country's in a mess.

All Are Bored

Commuters flocking to overcrowded trains.
We apologise for the interminable delay.
Weekend tomorrow, a temporary end to the pain.

Beach Amusements

Off to the beach, no space on the sand.
Time to hit the amusement arcades.
Fish and chips, wouldn't that be grand?

It's Not Just Cricket

Views from the pavilion.
Cover drives and square cuts for four.
Howzat - summer sounds for millions.

A Remembrance

Fall in for those who fell.
Poppies pinned to proud veterans.
All with stories, though some will never tell

Life After Television

I finally turned off the TV,
Said hurrah to ditching the remote.
Shuffled off the cushioned sofa
And did something else of note.

I read two books a week.
Wrote a poem or twenty three.
Cleaned the house from top to bottom
And made endless pots of tea.

I ran 5 miles each morning,
Walked at least 10,000 daily steps.
Spent 2 hours in a meditative state,
Lived each minute without regrets.

I wrote a brand new novel,
Learned to play the piano and drums.
Listened to every album on Spotify
And baked cakes and pies and buns.

I reupholstered all the furniture,
Learned Shakespeare's plays off by heart.
Mastered yoga, kung-fu and tai chi,
Woke up every morning, long before the larks.

Yes I finally switched off the TV,
Kettle's boiling for the umpteenth brew.
Yep, completed life, ticked that box
And now there's nowt left to do.

Now where is that remote...

This Generation

This generation
Is gonna walk with their heads held down
Staring at a screen, just above the ground.

This generation
Is gonna lose the power of speech
As they emoji, tap and text gazing at their feet.

This generation
Is just going to see the Earth
Through Instagram and Google photos, for what that's
worth.

This generation
Is not gonna know where they are
Unless they're told by Alexa or Siri or a Satnav in a car.

This generation
Will forget everything they learn or are told
For the sake of clicks and likes and constant scrolls.

This generation
Will regress to grunts and moans
Neanderthal postures, stooped over their phones.

This generation
Will wander, walk, spend lives alone
But with just one close friend,

A screen on a phone.

Phones in the Past

Why can't we go back,
To when phones were simply just phones?
A receiver, a spinning dial,
A single line into the home.

Standard ring tones,
And shrill clanging bells.
Who's ringing this time of night?
A time when no-one could tell.

A tall red telephone box
That ate all your loose change.
Where you stood waiting for your turn
For an hour in the cold and wind and rain.

A well-thumbed, dog-eared Yellow Pages.
Dialling 123 for the time from a clock that spoke.
Imbibing the smells of damp, musty, discarded fags.
Coughing and spluttering from the previous user's smoke.

Why can't we go back,
To when phones were simply just phones?
Not all YouTube singing, TikTok dancing, tweeting
Televisions, radios, computers, online banking zones.

When the news came from radio and telly.
When you bought books, records, everything in a shop.
When you just shrugged your shoulders and said oh well,
When whatever it was you wanted was no longer in stock.

Why can't we go back,
To when phones were simply a mode to talk?
Not permanently fixed with heads held down,
Eyes and fingers scrolling, unseeing where we walk.

Why can't we stop, switch off, think, disconnect,
And reclaim a little of the past?
When phones were simply just phones.
And if you needed to know an answer you'd have to ask

Someone, an encyclopaedia, a librarian, a teacher.
Your mother, father, grandparent, an intelligent friend.
Or simply pick up the phone and dial, wait, listen
And hope there would be someone on the end.

Followed by World Leaders

I was followed by Barack Obama,
As I browsed Tesco's Free From aisle.
I was followed by Joe Biden,
As I picked up a tasty apple pie.

I was followed by King Charles III,
As I loaded up on vegetable soup.
I was followed by António Guterres,
As I juggled tins of beans and spaghetti hoops.

I was followed by Xi Jinping,
As I perused a choice of shampoo.
I was followed by Kim Jong Un,
As I selected coconut scented paper for the loo.

I was followed by Elon Musk,
As I loaded my bags for life and paid.
I was followed by Donald Trump,
On just another ordinary day

Being followed by the great and the bad.
Being followed right around the shop.
Perhaps I'd better delete the Twitter app
Or else they'll never stop

Following me for the likes.
Following me for the retweets.
I wish they'd all stop following me,
So I can go home and eat.

We Were Once
(Ode to the 80s)

We were once
Tree climbers and
Carefree skateboarders,
Top Trumpers and
Marble hoarders.

We were once
Den builders and
Stay out till dark-ers,
Roll down the hill-ers and
Champion street footballers.

We were once
Record collectors and
Panini World Cup Stickers.
Record the top 40 singers and
Mixed C90 cassette compilers.

We were once
Countryside explorers on
Raleigh Choppers and Grifters.
Friday night fish n chip suppers
And rent a video Blockbusters.

We were once
Space Invaders zappers and
ZX Spectrum programmers.
Blue Peter and Swap Shoppers
Little Chefs and Happy Eaters .

We were once
Infants, children, teenagers,
Following fashions, it's all the ragers.

Heads in books and turn the pagers.
Dreaming big, all the world's a stagers.

We were once.
We close our eyes,
We are again.

Growing Up in the 80's
(One Album at a Time)

We were the *Kings of the Wild Frontier.*
The *Boy*-s who *Dare*-d, *Brothers in Arms,*
Ignoring *The Hurting,* sticking two fingers up at
Scary Monsters (and Super Creeps).

Such youthful exuberance ,
Human Racing and meeting girls.
Kissing to be Clever, such a
Wonderful Life, Human's Lib!

We were together,
Quick Step and Sidekick,
The Colour of Spring in
Sleepy *English Settlements.*

We made our *Declaration!*
Welcome to the Pleasure Dome.
So, Let's Dance to the *Spirit of Eden.*
Viva Hate? No, *It's My Life.*

We spent summer holidays
Beach bound in Eastbourne,
(Not *Rio*) and professed an
Inexhaustible *Lexicon of Love.*

We ate and drank, salad days,
Because yes, *Meat Is Murder!*
And promised we'd keep the *Faith,*
A *Synchronicity,* even if we *No Parlez.*

The heat meant *No Jacket Required.*
Hysteria on the *Road to Hell,*
As the summer raged and we made a
Promise to always remain *True.*

128

We danced to the *Non-Stop Erotic Cabaret*
In *Penthouse and Pavement* and read
Thriller-s about the *Disintegration* of society
And the *Ghosts in the Machine.*

And the years changed us as we grew
And started on new paths and *Strange Ways,*
Here We Come! *Signing Off* to begin
Our *Fantastic Labour of Love* with life.

Broken and Mended

Mary Green

Sun wakes me early: I open the window a crack
Not too far to chill the red begonias.
I drink tea and muse on broken china
I have them all over the house, mended jugs,
Glued together haphazard, not thrown away.
The Japanese value mended objects
More even than the pure unbroken ones,
I've found that they don't just cobble them together.
They use gold dust in glue, stick them with care
So they are more beautiful in their broken state,
Shining better than they did when they were whole.
Later I walk the canal. There by the motorway bridge
Next to the graffiti, there used to be a cherry plum.
It was cut down years ago, by accident they said.
My early spring shower of white disappeared.
Today I blinked. There it was again. Full white bloom.
It must have lived on underground and suckered up,
Quietly getting its strength till this cool spring
(A good year for cherry plum) it sprang back out,
More beautiful for having been missed so long.
Stronger for having been nearly destroyed.
I feel the gold dust in my belly, flowers in my eyes.
Maybe I too can be better mended. Maybe the world can.

café and carefree

Jim Young

sit me at a café table
with a book across your smile
coffee me and croissant me
we'll go that extra mile
we'll talk of yesterday
last night
the plans we have today
and when the papers say something awful
you look at me that way
you know ~ sort of quizzical
you smile at my smile
and we laugh the moment away

For you and me

John Lalitav

an old friend
centuries ago
wrote as the sun rose
as stars shimmered,
he wrote
for every cloud
and sky
for seas shifting
to and fro
and winds
breathing every tree
he wrote a whisper

he wrote for quiet times
for night
for day
for every sunflower seed
and acorn tree

he wrote for every heart - twinkling eye
he wrote for each and all
he wrote for you and me

his pen dripped a little ink,
signed his name, Issa

he wrote:

slowly, slowly
little snail,
Climbing Mt. Fuji.

Friendship

Jenna Plewes

A word, a smile, a hug
ripples spreading
lapping against the distant shore

cutting through slicks of sorrow and pain
rocking boats loaded with troubles
tugging at their anchors

setting the seaweeds swaying and dancing
bringing the sluggish backwaters into life

this is the gift of friendship

Good Air

Jerry Swartout

Good air
blows in freely
bringing everything we need
rain snow shade
with the clouds it made
the beauty it coveys
on grey overcast days, or
in crystalline blue sky
with cloud ships passing by.
Through transparent nights
when the depths of space
and the stars there
draw nigh
Good air
our breath
where we live
our life.

I Fell in Love With an Estate Agent

Simon Zec

He stood in the kitchen
White jeaned
Smart cardigan
Keys for his Jag luxuriating on the table

He showed me his karate moves
And the photo on his new i-phone
Of the x-ray of his broken finger

This fine figure of an early middle aged man
Full beard
Without a speck of grey
Quiffed fringe
With just a hint of length at the back

Lining up his clients
Placing them from home to home
Ensuring they move smoothly
Into their next multi-million pound mansion
For a one and a half percent cut

He looks at the hole in the wall
And spouts potential
The damp is an excuse for an extension

And the view!
Look at the view!
Just take away the old shed
And put in a seating area
You could drink your wine with him
Watching the sun set together

This man, an expert on the area
This man, an expert on building works
This man, an expert on 5g coverage
This man, an expert on proposed building in the area
This man, an expert, an expert, an expert

The tenants?
Don't worry about them
They'll be gone before the sale
No problems at all

The neighbours?
So friendly
No noises at all
The parking?
No problems
At all

Such reassurance
In such smart clothes

I want to fall into his arms
Nestle on his paunch
And swim in his confidence

Open-Eyed Prayer

Jenna Plewes

The soil is sliding into sleep
smelling of sun and heat
stored and swaddled
safe for spring.

I stand among the bean poles
falling sideways now
sticks and vine stalks
tangling courgette plants
their leaves crisp as toast.

A shadow moves across the field
a breeze ruffles the grass
a wash of sunshine
touches the wind-spinners
copper and steel catch the light
spiderlings float past
on threads tenuous as hope.

Smiles Ahead of Me

Rhianna Levi

Why I smile in the days of rapturous gloom is the thought
of seeing outside lava eyes flow in gold,
An event of favourite things coming to lilac for both me
and you.

I gracefully smile because of the songs cast across lakes in
my fresh eardrum,
Much like colloquial mellows of those before and
thereafter,
Listing all the reasons I belong here in day break's sweetest
enriched mug.

There are smiles that come from my Sunday baking
mishaps,
The psychoanalytical stories I witness and read across the
ghostly line.

All exalted reasons that I smile at the conclusion of the
day,
In midst of my hand-built bed of composure.
Prepared again to grin in the latest sleep play,
Directed by the brain gremlin who visits me at eve in silent
frames.

The Audacity of Hope

Mariangela Canzi

People lost to war.
People living all alone.
People with no food nor home.
People with no aim at all.

Hard life for those
Who cannot hope.

I will care for them.
I will put a flower
In their hands.
I will talk to them.

I, bright candle of Light,
I will give it to them.

The Photo In My Hutch

Madeline Heit Lipton

A wife sat as her Korean War Vet husband stood
Before their anniversary cake.
Not just any number, mind you
A 2 candle combo, amazing 68!

Genuine smiles and now older eyes,
Beamed pride into the camera lens.
A single photo from 2020, the extraordinary pandemic
year.

It was but one month after that simple click of the lens
I heard the unthinkable, unfathomable fact.
My Father, a brilliant, about to turn 90 years old, Korean
War Vet.
4th of July baby to boot, lover of life and family,
superhuman (or so we thought)
Was no more.
A text to be my goodbye.

One month after that simple click of a lens
I found myself reading 5 pages behind a mask,
His flag draped casket in back.

Remembering when he flew us up to the blue skies above
in his Piper Cherokee.
People down below waving him off, as if he was a
celebrity.
The time we saw his invention from long ago all over the
internet.

His beautifully built battery operated Model T Ford that
rode down our block.
Fitting two gleeful young children.
The Hilton brochure he graced the cover of
(So handsome was he on it)
Moments of a life, so well lived.
Mom handed me the Veterans flag.
Brother shared the fact that a heckuva lot of knowledge
would be lost on the world.

6 months later, grief mixed with happiness.
Spying a few strands of near 90 year old hairs stuck amidst
the headrest of his car.
I saved them, just glad that a personal piece of him can not
be taken away.

These are now new todays and tomorrows.
Believing my Father now has more sky to fly up in heaven.
That he is enjoying my Grandmothers phenomenal
cooking once more.
Reunited with those good people gone before.
Now I live with a knowing
That I can see his face in mine and on my children's too.
That I am blessed to be such a man's daughter.
And knowing when I need an extra visual
There is always that beautiful photo
Of a couple 68 years wed.
The photo in my hutch.

Fly high Dad.

THE VIEW FROM RYE HARBOUR

Henry Normal

A rainbow is best
over Dungeness
a mushroom cloud
and we're in a mess

TWO SUNSETS FOR THE PRICE OF ONE

Henry Normal

Ashen clouds
dwarf
the distant cliffs

Reflected in the shallows
the twilight adds colour to the marshlands
as their muted greens blacken

This immense canvas
is constantly retouched
around the Earth's curve

No composition could completely capture
the immediacy of this experience
it is beyond all five senses

Understandable when you consider
the size of the human eye
and the vast nature it tries to contain

Even a winter nightscape
with its limited pallet receding
surpasses imagination

York

Dean Wilson

York is full
of ghosts
I know a few
of them

sometimes
when I'm asleep
we meet up
and live again

I've not been
in a while
at least not
in the flesh

I'll return by
bus one day
when the walls
are daffodil blessed

Index of Poems

Title   **Page**

Note:
Sea Grief was inspired by the 2022 Welsh Children's Book of the Year, 'The Shark Caller', by Zillah Bethell (published 2020)
The Song Walker was inspired by Zillah Bethell's novel of the same name (published 2023)
The Depths was inspired by the Blue Peter Award winning writer Hannah Gold's 'The Lost Whale.' (published (2022)

Poems by First Line   **Page**

Guest Poem Contributors

Mariangela Canzi
Mariangela Canzi speaks Italian as her mother tongue and is a translator. Mariangela loves writing poems in English and is a regular contributor to the Poetry Review and Discuss Group on LinkedIn. Mariangela is honoured to be part of "Let the Acorns Grow." She strongly believes that sharing and caring are essential to everyone. Children and love must grow together.

Mary Green
Mary Green lives in Withybed Green, in the West Midlands, UK. She is happily retired after a career in further education, and spends her time immersed in and writing about wildlife and the environment, singing, writing poetry, growing fruit, and trying to keep up with the world. Mary helps to run the Withybed Poets. She believes everyone can make poetry.
Mary says,' Living in a village community in this part of the world is important to me and I am constantly amazed by the creativity of so-called "ordinary" local people.'

Rhianna Levi
Rhianna Levi is a writer, teacher and academic based in Worcester, England. She is a former Worcestershire Poet Laureate and is the 2023 Worcester Carnival Queen.
Alongside the publication of her debut poetry collection, Mortal Veins (2023), Rhianna has been published in numerous anthologies and literature mags. Rhianna has degrees from both the University of Worcester and Birmingham City University.
As a writer and holistic educator, her work empathises the complexity of humanity and existentialism that in itself is a remarkable phenomenon.

Facebook: Rhianna Levi
Twitter: @RhiannaLevi98
Instagram: @RhiannaLevi98

Madeline Heit Lipton

Madeline Heit Lipton is a writer, columnist and poet from the USA. She is a regular contributor to a number of magazines and publications and has been published in 8 books. Her poems are featured in the Poetic Bond, an annual anthology of poetry collating poetry from around the world on a variety of themes.

Henry Normal

Henry Normal is a writer, poet, TV and film producer, founder of the Manchester Poetry Festival (now the Manchester Literature Festival) and co-founder of the Nottingham Poetry Festival. In June 2017 he was honoured with a special BAFTA for services to television. He set up Baby Cow Productions with Steve Coogan in 1999, and was its managing director until his retirement in 2016.

Jenna Plewes

Jenna Plewes has published 6 poetry collections and one pamphlet. Her poems appear in journals and several anthologies. A Lick of Loose Threads, her latest collection, comes out later this year.(2023) and will be sold in aid of MSF. Her work as a psychotherapist and love of wild places gives her poetry its distinctive voice.

Jerry Swartout

Jerry Swartout lives in Hamilton, Montana, USA. He particularly enjoys 'haiku' poetry. He is a regular contributor to the Poetry Review and Discuss group on LinkedIn

Dean Wilson

Dean is a retired postman and lives in Withernsea in East Yorkshire. His books Sometimes I'm So Happy I'm Not Safe On The Streets and Take Me Up The Lighthouse are published by Wrecking Ball Press. His poems, videos and Pebble Of The Day can be found on Twitter @PoetDeanwilson6

John Lalitav
Almost 70 not older than 6, always better after drinking tea. Living in the north east with doggo and chum C.

Jim Young
Jim Young is a poet from Swansea, Wales, UK.
His poetry collections are available through his website, www.baitthelines.blogspot.com
Twitter, Jim The Poet @BaitTheLines

Simon Zec
Simon Zec is a Sussex based poet and tree surgeon. You can find him on Twitter at @SimonZec23 or on other socials too. His latest book In the Downtime is available from www.therealpress.co.uk or from Amazon His first collection Death of the Suburb is also available from the same places.

Authors Note

Thank you for buying A Promise of Hope.

With your support, Acorns Children's Hospice will continue to run their three hospices, in Birmingham, Walsall and Worcester, each of which is a lifeline for so many life limited children and their families.

To find out more about Acorns Children's Hospice and the work they do, as well as other ways in which you can support the charity, please visit their website at

www.acorns.org.uk

Acknowledgments

The following people have provided unstinting support and kindness, care and cups of tea in dark moments and bright. Thank you.

My wife Rini and daughter Louisa, always there for me. I love you very much. Keep smiling and inspiring. You are always my first and last thoughts of the day.

My mother Donna, our star baker extraordinaire, always served with a fresh cup of tea and a huge slice of love. My father Graham, brother Stuart and sister in law Rachel, my nieces and nephew Myrtle, Scarlett and Spike. Thank you for your kind words of love and encouragement that helped me in such dark times.

My Indonesian family. To Yangti, my wife's mother – always kindness in every smile. I have felt nothing but love and acceptance from the first time I arrived in Mranggen, central Java, Indonesia. Anto and Indah, Nina and Aris, Henny and Chandra and Heru and Wayhu - my brothers and sisters in law and all my nieces and nephews in Indonesia. Thank you. And to all my close and extended family and friends in Indonesia. *Terima kasih, marturnuwun sanget.*

To Acorns Children's Hospice. Your care and support for Milla when she was alive was exemplary. You became a part of our family. You were always there to help and guide us, take the pressure off us, allow us to rest and recharge our batteries. You were there for us when we lost Milla. You are there for us still.

Thank you for your constant support of my fundraising challenges. I am proud to represent Acorns as a parent, fundraiser and since August 2020 as an Acorns Parent Carer Champion.

A special thanks to Trevor Johnson, CEO for the foreword and to Noel Cramer, Director of Supporter Engagement for his continual kindness and support.

There are many who have encouraged my writing and poetry. In particular, Awais Khan, my friend and writer from Lahore, Pakistan. Thank you for words of wisdom, friendship and kindness and supporting my writing ambitions.

To Zillah Bethell, award winning author of The Shark Caller and The Song Walker, thank you for reading my work, for constant encouragement and telling me never to give up. Also to Hannah Gold, author of the award winning The Last Bear, The Lost Whale and Finding Bear, thank you. Your determination led to success and you inspire me to continue writing.

Thank you to Howard Linskey, Scott Fleming, Simon Zec, Jim Young, Dean Wilson, Rick Davis, Madeline Lipton, Mariangela Canzi, Trevor Maynard, Henry Normal, Brian Bilston, Francesca Martinez, Rhianna Levi, Monisha Rajesh, Tammy Gooding, Kate Justice and Malcom Boyden at BBC Hereford and Worcester, Kirstie Lynam, Catherine Mulvey and so many friends who have read my poetry over the years, as well as my two novels, The Shadows That Sang and Danny and the Last Rhinos. I have had so many words of encouragement, and every one was heart-felt and greatly appreciated.

Thank you to the poets who kindly allowed me to include one of their poems in this book.

Finally, to friends who know the difficulties we have faced a family, have witnessed the highs and lows, helped in the most terrible of situations. Lightened my mood with a kind word, or just company at the end of a phone, or in person. Your friendship is always valued, never taken for granted. Thank you.

Simon Whitton, Keith and Marilyn Crossland, Simon and Tracey Fraser-Clark, Fred Chevalier, Darren and Alison Faulke, Bob Whitelaw and Zoe Fisher, Dan Coll, Nathan Coll, Andy Fincham, Howard Gray, Jim Yeoman, Peter Stanley, Mike Stafford, Sean Beauchamp, Antony Bridge, Simon Deakin-Woods, Ellis Stewart, Oliver Groß, Sean Veasey, Neil Argue, Ian Kennett, Giles and Kathy Conlon, Shamoon Dean, AJ Crewdson, Luke Corbet, Andy Ingram, Alistair Falconer, Chris Burgess and Nikki Dennis, Kovan Bamarni, Simon Rothwell, Chris Munns, Mark and Debbie Langston, James Pascall-Smith, Karen Larkin, Claire Mould, Justin Shepstone, Simon Batten, Mark Anderson, Richie MacFarlane, Rick and Sue Johns, Chris Lynam,

Simon Lewis, Lorraine Bray-Cotton, Sian Spinney, Janette Peek, Jacqui Ferrett, David Wall.

My apologies to anyone I may have missed.

In loving memory of my daughters
Jewel and Milla.

The night sky is filled with myriad stars.
But I will always know where to look to find you.
The two brightest stars that light my heart and memory. Always.

About the Author

Anthony Frobisher lives in Worcester, UK with his wife Rini and daughter Louisa. In 2006, their triplet daughters, Jewel, Louisa and Milla were born 16 weeks premature. Jewel passed away after 17 days, but Louisa and Milla survived and after 6 months and operations on their eyes and on Louisa's heart, they came home.

Louisa is blind in one eye and partially sighted in her other. Milla had spastic quadriplegia cerebral palsy. She was unable to walk or talk and required feeding through a stomach tube and constant care. In 2016, Milla sadly passed away while on a trip to visit Rini's family in Indonesia.

Anthony turned to poetry to express his emotions and as a way to come to terms with losing Milla. He has not stopped writing since. He has written 16 poetry collections and completed two novels, The Shadows That Sang and Danny and the Last Rhinos, both set in Indonesia..

Anthony's poetry is available in Kindle download and paperback via amazon.co.uk (search Anthony Frobisher)

View Anthony's poetry on Instagram @ateafilledpoet and at www.frobipoetry.com

All proceeds from this book will be donated to Acorns Children's Hospice.

Thank you.
Anthony Frobisher
Worcester, June 2023

Printed in Great Britain
by Amazon

24547752R00089